The Lost Children

By
Brian J. Ek

Table of Contents

Foreword

There is no better feeling in the world like giving birth to a new baby. The feeling of having a child is wonderful especially when it is a healthy baby. However, the birth of a child with birth defects or other abnormalities is an entirely different story.

Imagine if you will. You give birth to a child that isn't quite as normal as you would like. A child with "Down syndrome", "Autism", "Cerebral Palsy" , or some other birth defect. The very thought is quite disturbing. According to cdc.gov, about 3 percent of new babies have birth defects that will require a great deal of care with costs for that care mounting to hundreds of thousands of dollars each year. This can be a huge financial burden for any family.

Imagine if your baby had these types of needs, what would you do? And as your child progressed in age, educating oneself with the care of your child can be mind-boggling too!

No one wants to think, what if. But there's still that chance that your new baby could suffer from a debilitating factor.

There's a lot more information out there these days than there were even thirty years ago, but that doesn't mean it's not still scary. Special needs children still need the love and care as a child with no health issues.

There is financial help from local, state and national agencies to help with the care of your child. Don't go it alone. Ask for help as it can go a long way in caring for your child.

More than seventy years ago, I had a relative that had a child with special needs. Little was known at that time about caring for children with special needs and most of these children were placed within state agencies or state hospitals.

One would think that would be a terrible thing to do. But with the lack of knowledge in the past, it was easier to place a child in an institution than to try and care for it oneself.

I remember my Dad telling me that he took this relative to Minneapolis to visit the child that he had placed in a facility for the first time in nearly fifty years. I could only hope that this first contact after so long a time had an impact for both the father and the child.

I couldn't imagine having to place a child in an institution these days, but it still happens.

Even when children reach an adolescent stage in life, children with disabilities or abnormal behaviors still get placed into facilities because parents just don't know what else to do.

In just the past decade, I decided to give back to the community and work in various settings. I've seen some very deplorable situations with these children and it's very upsetting for me. My heart hurts for these children, abandoned by their parents because of different circumstances.

Children brought to these facilities because of uncontrollable behavior, abandonment by their parents because of incarceration, alcoholism, parents that just don't know what else to do, because at some point their child won't listen any longer, birth defects like infantile alcohol syndrome and the like.

Most parents that are in their child's life, do care about the outcome of their child, however, not all parents think the same way.

Maybe the parent or parents have simply exhausted all of their resources as a parent and have thrown up their hands in frustration. Whatever the circumstances, it's important for the child to have their parents in their life.

Children need guidance and want to be told what to do. They need a mother and father to love them, regardless of issues that may be troubling in their lives. They need hugs on bad days and praise on great days!

Some children come from broken families and they usually are showing some behavioral issues extending from those circumstances.

I believe that many children need a framework and boundaries set up in the household in order for them to have some structure. Children also need to be able to be children. Some may not have any parents, due to death or incarceration or other extenuating circumstances, and they now have to be the adult, to care for their siblings.

I know... it's not really fair to think of a child having to take care of their younger siblings, but it does happen.

It's even harder to see those children in state institutions like regional treatment facilities, because their parents just forgot or decided not to be parents.

It's a given... children will push buttons of their parents and others to get their way. I've seen this time and time again.

Children want their way and will tell a parent what they want to hear in order to stop their children's behavior. It's an all too common practice, especially in toddlers and teens. Your child wants a toy in a store, you as the parent say "no", and the child has a negative behavior because of the parent's response.

Most always the parent's give in, because they don't want other people looking at them like a "mean" parent, thus causing the parent embarrassment.

In a case like this, it's important to stand your ground and not give in or talk to your child and reinforce the topic with, good behaviors will get rewarded. As I said before, children want to be told what to do and rewards for good behavior can be "key" to having a good relationship with your child. Giving in to your child's every whim can cause serious harm to your relationship as they will continue their bad behavior until you give in and give them what they want.

I think it's important to understand that no one is always going to be a "great" parent. I have certainly had my ups and downs in the art of child rearing. Everyone does have difficulty at some point during the raising of their child. And it's okay to slip and fall down. The important thing is to get back up and be steadfast.

There's no owner's manual when it comes to raising a child to become an upstanding adult. It's a trial and error thing. Being honest, truthful, caring and loving are the best things you can teach your child. But you'll need to be on your "guard". Deception is one thing your child will learn at a very early age. Playing one parent against the other is one of these deceptions.
Don't let this happen. Talk with your spouse and agree to you both making decisions for the betterment of your child. You both need to "nip it in the bud" together to make it easier for the both of you and your child. Your child will see that you both talk and make decisions together, thus your child won't play one against the other.

Getting back to regional treatment facilities... These facilities are mostly used as a last resort for children with negative behaviors. As I said, I've worked in a various facilities like these.

However, facilities like these are dwindling due to changes in our mental health governing bodies. Most of the facilities these days are more like incarceration for youth's ages 12 to 18, with little more for these children to do except sit in their rooms.

Restrictions on agencies like these and the staff that work within them are becoming very difficult because of rules like "245D", which creates guidelines that are more suitable for children, but mostly leave the staff feeling though their hands are tied.

A person can feel that the total safety for all those involved is compromised. Yet staff is expected to continue working and feeling like they're lives are placed in jeopardy on a daily basis.

Rule 245D is mind boggling for the state of Minnesota. If you don't believe me, take a look for yourself at: **https://www.revisor.mn.gov/statutes/cite/245D.02** .

It's getting harder for Direct Care Staff (DSP) or Mental Health Counselors to perform their job safely.

It is my belief that these rules need to be updated and the powers that be need to have the input of the people that work in the industry not only to make it safer for the people served but for the workers as well.

Some of the institutions where these children are seem to give these young people no direction. No punishment for bad behavior is allowed. They basically get the old slap on the wrist and are told not to do it again.

There's no clear effective way to teach these children right from wrong. No way to reprimand them for their bad choice. No way to hold them accountable for their actions.
Then, what are we teaching these children? That it's okay to lie, cheat, steal, beat up another child, simply because they want to? And yet not be held accountable for their action or actions?

It's truly not a realistic approach to child-rearing.

I do understand the reason why laws have changed. It's mostly caused from the children in some of these facilities that have decided that suicide is better than facing up to fact that they got in trouble or are in trouble and they see no clear way to make amends.

I don't take suicide lightly. I've had class mates and close friends that have decided that death is more important than life. It's a sad way to think of things. I've even contemplated it myself.

I've suffered from depression since childhood. It's a terrible thing to possess in one's mind... the thought that things would end and maybe those living wouldn't care too much that you weren't there any longer. This just isn't the mind set to have at any age.

I do believe that because of the multitude of suicides that the rules have changed.

Chapter 1.... What to expect as a staff

I've worked as a counselor in few settings and one that impacted my life the most was at a regional treatment center in central Minnesota.

My first few days were full of trainings. My first day on the unit was chaos. The reason I say this is that there seemed to be nothing set as far as a structure for these children or for the staff.

In some instances, I saw bullying by the staff towards the children. And then I saw it vice-versa. Wow! I was taken aback. Things immediately seemed to be in turmoil.

Each of the 4 units could house up to 12 individuals, and each unit housed individuals with different issues. Some of these units were for individuals with mental health issues, children in trouble with the law, behavioral issues and other concerns.

When I came to be onboard, the treatment center was for boys only. I heard horror stories of when the facility also housed girls.

The age ranges of the boys were from 12-18. Some if not most of them were medicated in some fashion.

I thought to myself, wow, what a crazy world within our world. How was I expected to make an impact on these children's lives?

I do have to let you know that since I worked at this facility, I had been contacted through Face Book by two young men that were in the facility when I was there. They both were very thankful that I had helped them with their problems and made a positive impact on their lives. I was simply beside myself after hearing that.

But I digress.

Being a part of the system was beneficial to me as well. It was my chance to "give back".

The facility was known to be faith-based, however, we were told to make no mention to "God" unless one of the children asked. Being an ordained minister, that was hard for me. The facility had a chapel on-site, but was closed.

I scratched my head in disbelief. Why then, if this was a faith-based facility wouldn't you have the chapel open to those that were interested in attending. I even volunteered to hold services for those interested. My gesture was never considered or responded to other than "the powers that be are considering it".

What a let down that was. So I decided to ask my supervisor if I could conduct Bible studies on the unit for those interested. He said yes, but a no pressure method had to be instituted. After all, we couldn't make it mandatory that individuals attended. We could only suggest that they could if they wanted.

Within the first week or two, I had started the Bible study. At first there were two or three boys who attended and each week one or two would join. I tried to supply Bibles if the unit library didn't have them.

Some of the boys attending didn't believe in God. I can understand completely. I looked through their eyes and thought, why would I believe in a higher being after looking at what my life is or has been. Why would "God" want anything to do with me?

For several weeks, the group delved into that question. I do remember one young man who accepted God as his savior. He actually got down on his knees and asked God for his favor and repented his sins.

From that time on, this young man flourished. The treatment center community was based on a four stage treatment. He was in level one and after accepting God, he continued to climb one level after another until he was finally released.

I remember the day that he left the facility. He came up to me and gave me a hug and he told me thanks for not giving up on him. I was really happy for him. Hopefully he is steadfast in his journey with God and on a clear path to recovery.

My supervisor took me aside and reminded me of the boundaries about no "hugging". I simply told him that I wasn't the one who instituted the hug. I also told him that if we open up as staff and become a little more vulnerable, it may help to get through to some of these children. He agreed, but told me to be careful.

That's the whole truth said right there. If we are more vulnerable, then maybe these children would let more of their guard down and start their recovery process a little easier. Who knows! Aren't the world's children worth it though?

During my first few months I witnessed many different behaviors. I was introduced to children's manipulation. It was their way of getting what they wanted. I also saw children playing one staff member for another.

Training supervisors made these behaviors out to be something new. I saw these behaviors as the normality of being a child and them trying to see which "buttons-pushed" to turn out for their benefit.

After all, these individuals are just that, "children". They all need guidance and support. This isn't rocket science here folks! So letting your guard down from time to time give them the understanding that you're no better than them and make them more comfortable to talking openly about their problems and issues, just like a child in your home.

I believe that asking questions of your child is the best way to know and understand their thinking process, rather than just guessing. Ask them how their day went, about adjusting to school, making friends for the first time. Be in their life; don't just sit idle amongst them. Be a parent. Besides, that's what you signed up for when you chose to have a child.

Training, training, training, that's what many of these institutions is all about. You really are expected to take a crash-course in mental health education and become a mental health counselor without the four-year-degree and license.

And the training was extensive to say the least. It went from learning how to use hand-cuffs, to understanding gang signs. I was taken aback on many occasions by the things I was being trained on.

All the staff was trained on medicine dispersal as well as first aid and CPR. If we made medicine dispersal errors three times, it was made clear to us that our positions would be terminated or we would have to retake the tests to be qualified in medicine distribution again.

There were lots of stressors on the staff. In the event of an incident with an individual, staff would have to document it and make the proper calls to all those concerned.

On many occasions, usually during staff shift changes, one or more of the boys would act out, knowing that the staff that had been working a 12-hour shift would have to stay until the behaviors were done. For some of the staff a 12-hour day would last a few hours longer.

I saw counselors (staff) be on the unit for only one day and quit. Other times I would hear of a staff go have a smoke and never return. It was a very trying experience being a counselor on one of these units, but with help from other staff, it was usually a lot easier to work there when you, yourself had someone to talk to about the stresses that would pop-up each day.

I guarantee that you will see tons of stress, but if you find a positive way to deal with that stress it becomes almost non-existent.

One of the most challenging things I found to be were the times when a boy would start calling you names and swearing profusely at you because of a frustration that they have.

One of things that I found out is that the behaviors weren't actually directed at you, but the occurred because of some event in their life. It could be that they seem mad at you because you remind them of someone who may have beaten them, caused them grief in some way, or someone they just don't like.

They aren't actually mad at you, unless of course, you've done something to them to make them mad at you.

However they may escalate into a behavior that puts them or you in imminent harm. If this happens, you may required along with your support staff, to place in the child in a physical hold so that they can't harm themselves, members of the staff or others that they may be in contact with.

This can be a very scary situation, but don't be dismayed. As long as you and your staff remain calm things can go smoothly. But if you become injured in any way, it's important for you to report the injury to a supervisor and get medical attention right away if the injury is serious.

You'll always want to reassure the individual that you are there to support them and the physical hold will be released when it is deemed safe for all parties.

Sometimes it's necessary to leave the individual alone, but within eye contact. During this time, it allows the youngster to be disengaged or allow them to "cool off" enough for them to de-escalate. Many times this may be the answer to better behavior.

I can't stress it enough not to take their behavior personally. They are at many times not mad at you, but mad at the circumstance that upsets them.

Negative behaviors could extend from a variety of issues including not being able to have a visit from family, winter storms, thunderstorms, and an argument with a sibling, other family member, teacher or peer. Under no circumstances argue with the child. No good will come of it.

Sometimes it's better to walk away and have another staff handle the issue. Don't become a target for negative behavior or worse, an injury when common sense should come into play.

If the crisis at hand becomes worse, and possibly starts a riot, then have another staff call 911. Drastic times sometimes call for drastic measures like locking you and your staff in an office to keep from harm. I've seen it happen. One child has a negative behavior and entices others to join them in continuing the behavior.

The best thing to do in this circumstance is to stay safe and call for back up.

Manipulation can be used by the individuals and also by the staff. In once circumstance I remember a staff that decided to take it upon themselves to offer candy for good behavior. This was a big no-no.

We couldn't make deals for good behavior. We had to teach these children "life-lessons". It's different when you have a job selling and your boss offers you incentives to sell more. With children, their minds are developing and using this type of reward doesn't usually maintain itself very long and they come to expect more with little or know effort on their part.

A point system for behaviors was in place at this particular facility. If a child kept their room clean and didn't have any major outbursts, they could benefit themselves by earning "unit-bucks" to spend on different items.

All of these children had "bins" of goodies that had been supplied by parents or that they had purchased for themselves while on outings. They could work by cleaning, doing dishes, and helping with food distribution and other menial tasks. Rewards of "unit bucks" were given for those tasks that were completed without issues.

Manipulation can be used by the individuals and also by the staff. In once circumstance I remember a staff that decided to take it upon themselves to offer candy for good behavior. This was a big no-no.

We couldn't make deals for good behavior. We had to teach these children "life-lessons". It's different when you have a job selling and your boss offers you incentives to sell more. With children, their minds are developing and using this type of reward doesn't usually maintain itself very long and they come to expect more with little or know effort on their part.

A point system for behaviors was in place at this particular facility. If a child kept their room clean and didn't have any major outbursts, they could benefit themselves by earning "unit-bucks" to spend on different items.

All of these children had "bins" of goodies that had been supplied by parents or that they had purchased for themselves while on outings. They could work by cleaning, doing dishes, and helping with food distribution and other menial tasks. Rewards of "unit bucks" were given for those tasks that were completed without issues.

It was a very good way to teach them the value of working for their pay. It was also rewarding for them as it gave them a sense of direction and worth.

Hard work by staff usually wouldn't be overlooked. Many staff received rewards of many sorts for their good judgment and help.

Chapter 2... Different Diagnosis

I have worked with many people over the years with a much different mental health problem than others. Doctor's will many times give "labels" for these problems.

Here is a list of just a few.

- Anxiety Disorders
- Attention-Deficit Hyperactivity Disorder (ADHD, ADD)
- Autism Spectrum Disorder (ASD)
- Bipolar Disorder (Manic-Depressive Illness)
- Coping with Traumatic Events
- Depression
- Disruptive Mood Dysregulation Disorder
- Eating Disorders

It's often hard to be a teen, especially with all the opportunities presented to our children. Some children are born with mental disorders while others are not.

Anxiety disorder is a problem both in teen and adults. And being able to control it is sometimes very difficult.

My first wife had cerebral palsy and was prone to having severe seizures. Anxiety had a tremendous roll in her life. She could feel a seizure coming on and then would get anxious about it which would usually make it worse with a quicker onset.

I decided one day to try an experiment which I deemed to cause no harm to her. I suggested to her that when she felt a seizure coming on, to repeat, "I'm fine". I told her to say it out loud and keep repeating it over and over until the feeling of having a seizure passed.

I must say that I was totally surprised that she was able to keep that seizure from rearing its ugly head. And she was astonished that she could do this as well.

It's amazing what we can tell our brains to do. I'm very claustrophobic especially when it comes to tight spaces like an MRI machine. Sometimes I can talk myself out of climbing in, while other times I can talk myself into climbing in.

I believe that it's very important to mentally prepare oneself for any circumstance that one feels uncomfortable with. It really all depends on how well you prepare yourself.

People with anxiety concerns have often had some event in the past that has created this feeling of anxiousness. For me it happened when I was a child. I went ice-fishing with my Dad and 3 older siblings. I saw a car driving on the ice and then go through. No one emerged from the icy waters. That gave me what most physicians would call "PTSD" or Post Traumatic Stress Disorder, which is the same affliction that many of our military people experience.

It's an incredible uneasy feeling and can leave someone paralyzed in more ways than one.

It's very important to recognize PTSD and Anxiety Disorder as real. But its how one copes with the problem that changes can be made to deal with the disorder.

(ASD) Autism Spectrum Disorder was kind of a scary topic for me. This disorder is very broad, in the sense of having so many different symptoms and mannerisms.

I've worked with several individuals over the years with ASD. I was even told by a young man once when he was having a difficult time adapting to something, "I'm Autistic". I replied, you may be autistic, but you're not stupid!

My statement somehow made a connection for the both of us. And even though I don't work with this young man any longer, he still keeps in contact with me.

The important thing to remember is that if you can find a similar interest with someone that is autistic, you may have the ability to communicate on their level and make a connection.

Although I may discuss some of these mental health issues in this book, I can only base my findings on people with certain disorders. I don't have a degree in these fields and can only give my opinion based on my experience. I don't have experience with other disorders and cannot give opinions on those disorders that I've not dealt with.

If you would like to get more information on these and other mental health disorders, I urge you to visit The National Institute of Mental Health at: **https://www.nimh.nih.gov/index.shtml** . This is a great site to help both the aspiring mental health worker and a parent that would like to gain more knowledge about certain forms of mental disorders.

Chapter 3... After the Diagnosis

Much of the time after a doctor has diagnosed a child with a mental health disorder, parents often don't believe their child could have a disorder. What I'm saying is that they are in disbelief and may have that deer in the headlight look.

A parent may choose to deal with the issue themselves "head-on", while others may choose to throw their hands up and surrender, thus giving up being a parent to the child. It's a sad thing if a parent chooses the latter.

I've seen this first hand. A child will be placed in a setting of a mental health facility or group home. Visits by the parents will be set up and shortly thereafter a wealth of excuses will ensue. Excuses like "we can't make it today, something else has come up or I'm just not feeling that well today".

Then at that moment you see the child's face and their actions become grim. They know that their family is maybe embarrassed by having a child in a setting such as this or just giving up on them all together. It's a very sad choice by the parent.

Many times the parents feel as though they can't care for their child, while at other times it's too much of a financial burden. Whatever the case may be its child abandonment at its worse.

It's a terrible thing for a child not to have their parents in the picture. And children start to measure their own self-worth.

I've heard conversations from parents stating that it's just too difficult for them to deal with their child's behavior or that they have children at home too and they feel overwhelmed by adding a child with troubles into the scenario.

It is something that leaves scars on the child. And sometimes those scars may appear on the outside as well, Scars in the form of "cutting".

According to Webmd.com, Cutting is a practice that is foreign, and frightening to parents. It is not a suicide attempt, though it may look and seem that way. Cutting is a form of self-injury -- the person is literally making small cuts on his or her body, usually the arms and legs. It's difficult for many people to understand. But for kids, cutting helps them control their emotional pain, psychologists say.

I spoke to a young man about his reasons for cutting and he told me that it helped him deal with the fact that his parents were non-existent. He went on to say that if he hurts inside due from one thing or another that it helps him not feel as much hardship on the inside if he cuts himself.

This young man, through counseling along with staff's involvement helped him quit cutting and get on with his life in a positive way.

Sometimes the hurt on the inside has a long lasting effect. But when it comes to those that come to a child's aid like counselors and staff, where the child opens up and tells what their feeling, the hurt can be temporary.

Often children may be diagnosed with a mental health disorder when the child is only figuring out where he or she is in regards to their own sexuality.

This is often a topic that was taboo to talk about as staff. I believe this because mostly of sexual predators and pedophilia. Unfortunately there have been staffs that have taken advantage of children's diagnosis by engaging in sexual situations with them when a child is most vulnerable.

Personally I would like to see those people horse-whipped. It's terrible to prey on any child regardless of their mental health. It just makes me sick.

A young man that I was supposed to mentoring for anger issues came up to me one day and told me that he wanted to be a woman. I honestly didn't know what to say or how to deal with it.

I told him that I wasn't educated in this and he'd be better off talking with a psychiatrist than me. He told me that he wanted to talk to me as I was easy to talk to. Frankly I told him, that it just wasn't a topic that I knew anything about and felt very uncomfortable talking about it with him. After all he was in the facility for having anger concerns not sexual health concerns. I just told him that I couldn't talk to him about this topic and it crossed too many boundaries.

He tried on many occasions talking about it and I kept up my boundaries and declined.

I spoke with my supervisor on countless occasions and he finally had an appointment set up between a psychologist and the young man.

After a few appointments the young man came up to me and apologized for giving me such a hard time about talking about his sexuality. He also said that he appreciated getting the appointments set up with the psychologist because he was getting the answers he needed.

Being caught off-guard can be confusing at times for staff, but being truthful with a child and not acting like a know-it-all can be more beneficial than one would think. If you claim to be a know-it-all, then I would rethink about being a DSP or mental health counselor.

I could probably tell you hundreds of stories about different diagnosis and treatments but I won't. I think that it's more important to help you come to terms as a parent or staff on your own.

These children with mental health concerns can be mounting with no release in sight for a child. At least we as parents and staff have it within our grasp to help them out to the best of our ability. If you don't know something then talk to someone who does. Don't assume that just because you don't know the answer, which nobody knows.

Don't offer any knowledge if you don't have it, as it will most often land you in the "dog-house".

Chapter 4... Treat the person not the disorder

Unless you are a licensed professional, don't try and treat the symptoms or disorder as it is not your job. Treat each person with respect and dignity. Your job as a staff is simple. You are there for support.

Many times I found myself as a "sounding-board" to those I served. More often than not, an individual would come to me to "just talk". Maybe I in some way looked or sounded like I might be easy to talk to. The important thing here is to listen to their views and statements. Repeat things to them that you hear. For example; "so if I understand correctly what you're telling me, you believe that breakfast is really not the most important meal of the day, is this right"?

The best thing you can do is to stay attentive to their opinions and views. It's important to them and should be important to you.

I've been expected to read a manual or history of everyone individual I've had to come into contact with. I confess that it's a lot of reading. I chose to observe instead. I've found that observing is important to getting an understanding what I'm up against. Reading the history may be important as well. For instance; there may be harmful behaviors or triggers that could set off a series of harmful behaviors that cause a major crisis on the unit. So be tuned in to each individual whether reading or observing. And don't ever let your guard down to the point where you place yourself or someone else in jeopardy.

Maybe an individual that you are mentoring likes to talk about their mental health disorder, and how they agree or disagree with the diagnosis. You can speak about it, but just be careful that you don't cross the line about being a professional and thinking that you know more than the doctor about.

Doctors have many years of education and experience, whereas you might have some education, moreover you may not have the experience that doctors have. Be cautious and don't give advice but suggestions on how to cope with the affliction.

Coping skills are most often very helpful to reduce stress in a stressful situation. An example of a coping skill might be going for a walk, listening to music, using a stress ball or something else. It's always great to know what coping skill the individual enjoys the most. The coping skill can be your best friend at times when the potential of a negative behavior might exist.

"Triggers" are another thing to keep in mind as well. A trigger could be something that comes to mind that triggers a behavior. It could represent itself in many different forms. Maybe you look like a parent that beat their child or you remind them of someone that threatened them in the past. A trigger could be a motion or movement made by you or someone else. Just know your surroundings in case you have to make a fast getaway if a negative behavior occurs. Maybe have extra staff come into the picture.

You'll also need to know this. Don't crowd the individual. If you have someone that is experiencing negative behavioral tendencies, sit down with them if you can and discuss all the options. Have other staff be on standby in the background, ready to intervene at a moments notice. Don't ever stand over an individual as they may perceive this as a threat. Be just as concerned with the issue as they are. This will show that you truly care. Children can see through you if you don't share with them that you care, and the outcome of this won't be pretty.

The most important thing is to listen and repeat what they're saying and don't look around, but look at them while they're talking. This will most often get you off the hook at becoming a trigger. However, if you look away, they will commonly figure that you're not interested in helping.

If the individual goes to the wall and starts banging their head against it, this is most often a sign that want someone to intervene and speak with them. It's not the time to perform a physical hold unless you're instructed by a supervisor or higher up. If the child becomes aggressive towards a staff or peer and attacks them, then is the time for a physical hold.

Make no bones about it. You'll know along with your staff of the time that a physical restraint needs to be engaged. And it's important to discuss with your team the appropriate time to institute a physical restraint. This is only to be used as a last resort. It's also important to know if the individual in question is "hands-on" or not.

Rest assured that you will most always receive extensive training in this department and be sure to always ask questions, even if you think you know the answer. It's better to know the complete picture than to not know it completely and lose the ability to come to work the next day or be out of a job.

It's always a positive thing to let the individuals in your care know that you care about them. Build trust as solid as a rock and don't deviate from that. It's important for them to know that you are there for them at a moments notice. Set up boundaries, don't divulge too much about your personal life unless you feel totally confident that no lines in safety will be crossed. After all you are just as human as the ones in your care. Be honest and upfront with them and the trust will be earned by both parties involved.

Don't ever promise something that you can't see to fruition. Broken promises are very difficult to come away from when it comes to trust.

Try to find things that the child and you have in common like fishing, hunting, sports or just the great outdoors. This may be beneficial to both of you.

If you are able to go on a safe "outing" with them, ask them their interests and desires. It's important for them to feel as though their feelings are of interest to you. This will help build a bond between you and the child.

While on the outing, talk about things that maybe they've done in the past that they enjoy.

If your supervisor deems it safe, and your child shares and interest in fishing, then take them fishing and talk about topics that are appropriate to fishing. Things like what kind of bait they like or what kind of fish they've caught or like to catch. Are they a catch-and-release type of fisherman or if they want to keep and eat their catch.

I remember taking several individuals out fishing on a boat and during our trolling on the lake, a young man snagged a monster pike. When he finally reeled it in to the boat, he was very careful about removing the hook and placing it back in the water by moving it forward and backward until he finally released it. I made the comment about his commitment to seeing that the fish was healthy enough to be released. He smiled.

It's moments like this that truly gave me a warm feeling of admiration for those young people. He felt great about my compliment and I in turn had a great feeling for him.

These moments are very stimulating and therapeutic and give these folks a chance to forget about their afflictions for even a small amount of time.

It's also times like these that I may have needed a chance to unwind and relax doing something that I enjoyed just as much as those in my care at the time.

As I've stated earlier, I've had a few young men that were in my care contact me through social media.

One of those young men comes into mind that lost his mother due to an illness. He had never mentioned his father to my knowledge and his mom was his world.

It was a few years later that I learned of her passing. I expressed my sympathy to him while talking on the phone. He stated that he felt better about himself after the treatment center. He also stated that he was sorry for giving me such a hard time and also expressed his admiration and thankfulness that I never gave up on him. He went on to say that if he could ever have a Dad, he would want him to be just like me.

I have to confess that I had tears in my eyes with that comment. It felt so wonderful that I had made an impact in his life.

One of the other young men that I mentored also contacted me through social media. He was working in the Minneapolis are as a tow truck driver and wanted to know if he could come and see me. I told him that would be great.

He came up to see me on Father's day a year or two ago. He and I talked about the good ole days while he and I were at the treatment center. He admitted that he was now better because of my continued interest and support.

He came from a family of divorced parents and had issues of anxiousness on many occasions.

He stated that my help getting him through those times helped him tremendously. He was able to secure a job and keep it, even though some of the jobs he had in the past didn't work out because of his loss of interest.

He then spoke more about helping others like I had helped him. I asked if he was available to do some work around my home if I'd pay him. He was very interested and came to my home on more than one occasion. He laid mulch and helped me build a deck. He told me that it was "cool" that he now knows how to build a deck. I told him that this is the way I learned, by watching someone else. He was pleased and would call on occasion and ask if I needed more help.

Again, times like these are very heart-warming for me. It's great to think that I made a friend and an impact on his life.

Chapter 5... Faking the treatment

It's great to have those that went through the treatment with success, but there were individuals that "faked" their treatment in order for them to get out of the treatment center setting, only to come back again.

I remember a few of those that did this. After all, no one wants to be told what to do.

One of these young men faked his treatment, only to be moved to a foster home setting and on his first night steal his foster parent's vehicle. It's really sad, because I saw that this young man as a good kid. His parent's were pretty much not in his life. His mother was a prostitute and his father was no where to be known.

He did however seem to have close ties to his grandparents. This young man had a vision of owning his own mechanic shop and the rebuilding of old cars. He seemed to be quite knowledgeable in this field. He would often talk about rebuilding an old vehicle with his grandpa on a farm.

This young man seemed to be on-board with the treatment process and cruised along through the levels of getting released.

I built a rapport with him and in his own mind he became one to stand up for me in the event of trouble with other youth.

To expressed to him my gratitude but told him that I was entirely able to stand up for myself. He understood, but came to the aid when he saw trouble brewing.

Back in the day before rule 245D, the presence of calming rooms were available for those individuals that were incorrigible. These rooms were present in the event that an individual needed to be separated from the rest of his peers in a controlled environment. The door usually had a small indestructible window in it and device with a magnetic lock and button.

This room was used many times to help calm down troubled folks. I tried being in the room myself and found it to be very disturbing to me and made me feel very claustrophobic. So I could see why these went away with the implantation of 245D.

I witnessed many young individuals cooped up in these small rooms. Some people it actually helped while others it didn't help at all. Sometimes the youngsters would go into the room and just sit on the floor as there were no furnishings for safety's sake.

I've seen both positive and negative results from using this room. But enough has been said about this topic as it is no longer lawful to use it.

The number one thing for me to get into the brain of someone I mentored was to let them know that this was a "start over point" for them. It was a chance for them to learn about themselves and others and help them to become outstanding citizens. However in many instances this didn't work as some of the children involved had nothing to go back to when they were released.

Some of them had no families, or were in gangs, or just had no one to turn to in order for them to get access to food, shelter, clothing or other needs. Many of these folks had to rely on themselves to stay alive especially if they were living on the streets. It's a sad alternative to not having families who care.

I saw many Native Americans that were adopted by Caucasian families only to be turned away when the going got tuff. Or some of these individuals had hope of returning to the only families they ever knew, gangs.

That's why it's so important to care for the children. Whether from a parental standpoint or from a staff, it's vital that care is taken to prevent potential negativity from being placed on our youth.

It's imperative to instill good healthy habits like taking care of oneself both physically and mentally. Even if the young person has issues in these fields, they should be addressed at the earliest sign.

If you see and individual "faking" his or her treatment, let them know that you see through it. This is sometimes the only technique you can use to help them change their view. And again, showing that you are truly concerned with their well being is key.

Chapter 6... How can I help as a caregiver?

Realistically it's more important to just be yourself when it comes to working with and for individuals with mental health disorders. Don't fake it. As I stated earlier in this book, the ones you care for will see right through you.

Learn as much about the individuals as you can. You want to help in any way you can otherwise you've chosen the wrong job.

Is it scary? Yes! It's because of this fact that this field sees so much turnaround in employees. You will need to have strong nerves much of the time. But the positive benefits to your position will out-weigh the negatives in most cases.

Remember to stand your ground but also open up and listen to those you serve. It may be a long and hilly road, but the outcome can be very educational and worth every penny you've invested in helping the betterment of the child. This goes for both the parent and the staff. Staff in many ways appears to the individual as a parent.

Learn to be a good listener. I've failed in this in my marriage and to this day have issues with it. But this too can be overcome. Let these children know that they can trust you with their most intimate details about their life.

Be sure not to share details about one child's life to another. First of all you violate "HIPPA" rules and you also violate the trust of the child.

Don't be afraid of rejection. I've never been able to be accepted by a stranger on the spot. This is something you'll need and want to work on. Find a common interest and build a rapport. Only then will the possibility of trust come into play.

Don't ever be afraid to ask questions. As you've probably heard before, the only dumb question is one that has yet to be asked. You don't need to be afraid of the individual you are serving. Ask as many questions as you need to get a better understanding of who you're dealing with. And further, be prepared for the answers. Some of those answers might not be too pleasant.

If you haven't totally committed yourself to working in this field, then I urge you to watch a movie entitled; Short Term 12. According to Wikipedia the film is 2013
American **independent drama film** written and directed by **Destin Daniel Cretton**. It is adapted from Cretton's **short film** of the same name, produced in 2009. The film stars **Brie Larson** as Grace Howard, a young supervisor of a group home for troubled teenagers. The film was the first leading performance of Larson's career.
Cretton based *Short Term 12* on his own experience working in a group facility for teenagers. He first wrote and produced a short film exploring this and later adapted it into a **feature-length** screenplay. While Larson and **John Gallagher, Jr.** won their roles after auditioning through **Skype**, most of the children featured in the film were cast through open **casting calls**. Filming took place over twenty days in **Los Angeles**, **California** in September 2012.

Short Term 12 premiered on March 10, 2013 at **South by Southwest**, where it won the Grand Jury and Audience Awards for a Narrative Feature. The film was theatrically released in the United States on August 23, 2013, by **Cinedigm**. Made on a budget of less than $1 million and given a **limited release**, the film brought in strong box office receipts, grossing over $2.3 million.[2] Critics praised its realism and intimacy, and especially Larson's performance and Cretton's screenplay and direction. The film is considered one of the best of 2013, appearing on several critics' year-end lists. It was listed by the **National Board of Review** as one of the **Top Ten Independent Films** of 2013. It earned three **Independent Spirit Award** nominations, including **Best Female Lead** for Larson.

This was introduced to me by a coworker and is probably the best introduction for working in this field that I've ever come across. Even though I had already chosen to work in this area, I still found it to help me with everyday life on the job.

Another thing I should mention is that many young individuals will use this statement projected towards you that, "He's only working here to collect a paycheck". While this is true unless you're financially stable where you don't need a paycheck, you should never agree with the statement. If you do, you will never attain any level of respect from anyone.

Don't challenge an individual, don't seek out a fight. If the opportunity arises, walk away. Don't challenge the opinion of a coworker in the immediate presence of a "client" or someone you serve. Take the coworker aside to a private location and discuss your concerns. It's important to remain professional in the presence of the one you are caring for.

If you see something that just doesn't seem right or ethical to you when dealing with another staff, take them aside or contact your supervisor. Not every staff will see things your way and if you have a higher ethical standard it's sometimes better to get things straightened out when working with a client.

Here's a word that I really don't like to use, "Client". You're working with a real live breathing person and I have issues calling them clients. It seems demeaning to me to use that term. Maybe it's just my thinking and you may have no issues with the term. I on the other hand would rather call them people I care for.

Don't ever engage in a "power-struggle". The person you serve is basically testing the waters and pushing buttons to see how far they can control you or the situation. If you see this becoming an issue, then walk away and say, what don't you take some time to think about your feelings and get back to me. This gives you the option to discontinue the conversation safely and leaves no doors open other than re-discussion later.

In Closing

If I've done nothing more than to educate you on working in a healthcare field, I've what I've set out to do. I also wanted to be sure to give potential or existing parents some insight to what I've seen while working with so-called troublesome children.

We all have had issues in our life, but overcoming those challenges make us better, because we're telling those challenges to take a hike. Even to this day I have anger issues that seem to control me at times. I have to choose to overcome this challenge not only for me but for those around me.

There is no such thing as a perfect parent but there is such a thing called parenting. Choose to become a responsible parent when you choose to become a parent and raise your child to the best of your ability. You'll make mistakes, but you can choose not to make those mistakes over and over. Have faith in your abilities as a parent. Ask others for their input if you just can't seem to figure something out. It's not rocket science, if it were we would probably have a lesser population on planet Earth.

Face your fears head-on whether a parent or caregiver and don't let our offspring become the lost children.

"The Lost Children" by Brian J. Ek is a manual if you will, that was written with the Direct Service Provider or "DSP" in mind. Brian has no college education in this field, only his hands-on experience and years of training by mental health professionals which enabled him to write this book. Brian's opinions on topics described in this book are simply his own opinions and he in no way is a mental healthcare physician. This book is designed to help prepare oneself to work in the mental health industry for caring individuals and parents that want to make a positive impact in the lives of the children they work with.

If you would like to have me come and speak for your organizational event, please contact me via my email at: **bemgvoice@gmail.com**